D1278217

MAP MATH

Math and My World

Kieran Walsh

Rourke
Publishing LLC
Vero Beach, Florida 32964

www.rourkepublishing.com

PHOTO CREDITS:
Cover photo by Corbis.com. All other photos from AbleStock.com, except for p. 5 by the author and illustration of man and woman with giant compass © Getty Images

Editor: Frank Sloan

Cover and interior design by Nicola Stratford
Page layout by Heather Scarborough

Library of Congress Cataloging-in-Publication Data

Walsh, Kieran.
  Map math / by Kieran Walsh.
     p. cm. -- (Math and my world)
Includes bibliographical references and index.
Contents: Scale -- The compass -- Globes, longitude, and latitude --
Elevation -- Depth -- The solar system.
  ISBN 1-58952-379-2 (hardcover)
 1. Mathematics--Study and teaching (Elementary)--Juvenile literature.
2. Cartography--Juvenile literature. [1. Mathematics. 2. Cartography.]
I. Title. II. Series: Walsh, Kieran. Math and my world.
  QA135.6.W322 2003
  912'.01'4--dc22
                                    2003011557

Printed in the USA
w/w

TABLE OF CONTENTS

INTRODUCTION

People use maps all the time, and for good reason. Maps make it easier to find out where you are and how to get to where you want to go. This is called **navigation**, the process of directing cars, boats, airplanes, and even people.

When was the last time you used a map to get somewhere? Can you think of ways that math relates to maps?

If you ever find yourself in a big, unfamiliar place like a park or a train station or a shopping mall, the simplest way to orient yourself is to find a map. Often times, even the spot on the map where the map actually *is* will be labeled clearly as "you are here."

Maybe you never knew it, but maps depend on math for their accuracy. You see, most maps are created to help people travel great distances. Because of this, the details on a map have to be precise. It is math that guarantees this precision.

It's pretty difficult to get lost anywhere as long as there are maps around. This map shows a portion of downtown Manhattan, New York City.

SCALE

Maps are like pictures that show you places and things from angles that you would probably never see in real life. The most common angle for a map is a view from far above, which is sometimes called a "bird's eye view."

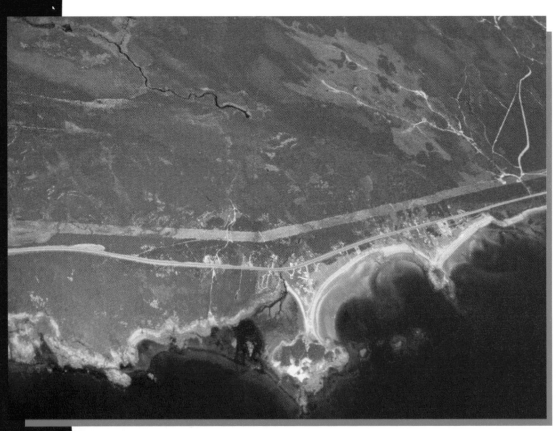

In one sense, a map is simply a picture taken from a point of view you might not see otherwise. This aerial view of a highway, for instance, looks very much like a road map.

On the other hand, a map is much more than just a picture because it is meant to show very specific information. Photos of North America taken from spacecraft don't look much like maps. For one thing, the states aren't divided and labeled. Roads are not highlighted. Also, the capital of each state isn't marked with a star.

To sum up, a map is like a picture, but it is a picture meant to convey specific types of information like **distance**. Calculating distance is one of the most common uses for a map. Maps make this an easy task because they are drawn to **scale**.

What does that mean, drawn to scale?

Essentially, it means that the subject the map represents is, in reality, a different size. This is done mainly for practical reasons. For example, a map of the United States that was the same size of the United States wouldn't be very useful. To start with, you wouldn't be able to store it anywhere!

Instead, people rely on maps that depict large areas on a smaller scale. In other words, maps use exact measures of a smaller length to stand for exact measurements of a larger length.

Have you ever wondered how "big" the United States is? You can find out by using a map.

Your map of the United States might use a different scale, but for the purposes of this example, imagine that the scale of the map is 1 in. = 150 mi. (1 inch equals 150 miles.)

Using a ruler, find out how many inches there are between the West Coast of the United States and the East Coast.

Your map might be different, but in this case, let's say there are about 18 inches from the West Coast to the East Coast. To convert this distance from inches to miles, all you have to do is multiply the number of inches by the scale:

$$18 \times 150 = 2700$$

So the United States is about 2,700 miles across!

Now that you know the distance of the United States *across,* what about the distance from top to bottom?

This is a little trickier than measuring the distance across, because this time there isn't a specific stopping point like the Atlantic and Pacific oceans.

Instead, let's concentrate on what is probably the longest distance from the top to the bottom. This is most likely from the northern border of the United States with Canada to the southern border with Mexico, through Texas. Let's say that distance is about 10.5 inches. What is that distance in miles?

$$10.5 \times 150 = 1575$$

So there are about 1,575 miles between the northern and southern borders of the United States!

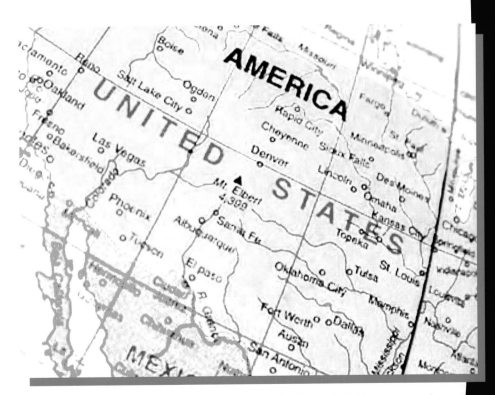

Scale varies from map to map, but if you do the calculations correctly, you should come up with a number of approximately 4.2 million square feet for the total land area of the United States.

Now that you have those two calculations, you can even calculate the **area** of the United States. That is to say, the measure of the total land mass.

To calculate this figure, you need to multiply the distance across by the distance from top to bottom. The results will be in square miles:

$$2700 \times 1575 = 4252500$$

So the total area of the United States is about 4,252,500 square miles! To make things simpler, you can also round that number down and say that the total area of the United States is about 4 million square miles!

As you can see, maps are very useful for measuring distances, which is why they come in handy when planning a trip. **Direction** is another reason why maps are so useful. It's good to know how far away your destination is when you begin a trip, but unless you know what direction to travel in, you might as well stay home.

Legends

Very detailed maps often come with legends. A **legend** is a box on the map, usually placed in one of the corners, that explains what the symbols—also known as icons—used on the map mean.

Some standard map icons include:

- ▲ - Triangles to represent mountains
- ● - Dark circles of varying sizes to represent cities of different populations
- ⧇ - A plate, knife and fork to indicate places where food is available

Can you think of other symbols that might appear on a map legend and what they would stand for?

What do you think the icon for a bridge would look like on a map?

THE COMPASS

Did you know that the earth itself is a giant magnet? Like a magnet, the earth has a North Pole and South Pole. The North Pole is usually referred to as the Arctic. The South Pole, on the other hand, is called Antarctica.

It is because of the earth's magnetic properties that people can use compasses. With the right maps and a compass, you can find your way just about anywhere in the world.

The information it provides is complex, but the compass itself is a very simple instrument.

A compass is an instrument that you are probably already familiar with, even though you may not understand how it works. Like the earth itself, a compass is also a magnet. More specifically, the directional needle on a compass is a small magnet. One end of the needle is usually painted. The needle revolves in reaction to the earth's magnetism, and the painted end always points north.

A typical compass indicates the four basic directions:

N – North
S – South
E – East
W – West

These directions always point in the same way:

North – Up
South – Down
East – Right
West – Left

North is always changing, but with North defined, you can also determine which direction is South, East, or West.

If you look more closely at the compass, you will see that it is also labeled with numbers. These are **degrees** of direction. Degrees are a unit of measurement developed by the ancient Greeks. They divided a circle into 360 portions, or degrees. Degrees are like very thin slices of a circle.

In order to understand degrees, it might help you to imagine a circular type of food, like a pizza or a cake, sliced into very thin pieces. There are 360 degrees in every circle. Can you imagine how thin 360 slices of pie would be?

What are the degree markings on a compass?

North - 0°

East - 90°

South - 180°

West - 270°

Let's try some math using these numbers. What is the difference in degrees between East and North? You can find out by using subtraction. Just subtract the smaller number from the larger number:

$$90 - 0 = 90$$

What about East and South? What is the difference in degrees there?

$$180 - 90 = 90$$

South and West?

$$270 - 180 = 90$$

You have probably begun to notice a pattern here. The difference in degrees between each of the four directions is exactly 90 degrees. These numbers are all **multiples**. More specifically, they are multiples of 90. You can see this for yourself if you divide any of the directions by 90:

$$\text{East: } 90 \div 90 = 1$$
$$\text{South: } 180 \div 90 = 2$$
$$\text{West: } 270 \div 90 = 3$$

Finally, you will notice that North is labeled 0 degrees. North can also be thought of as 360 degrees:

$$\text{North: } 360 \div 90 = 4$$

This is because 0 is sort of like a starting point. In order to make one full turn, or **revolution**, you have to travel from 0 degrees, to 90 degrees, to 180 degrees, to 270 degrees, and finally to 360 degrees, which is really returning to zero. Have you ever spun yourself around in a circle? You didn't know it at the time, but you were actually spinning your body 360 degrees, which is one complete revolution!

Things that travel in a circular motion, like this Ferris wheel, travel in terms of degrees. If one full revolution of the Ferris wheel is equal to 360 degrees, how many degrees are there in a half revolution? A quarter?

Some compasses also include four other directions, which are really just combinations of the first four:

NE – Northeast
NW – Northwest
SE – Southeast
SW – Southwest

You already know that the number of degrees between North and East is 90. How many degrees, then, is Northeast?

Since Northeast is a combination of North and East, it is exactly halfway between North and East. So, the degree measurement for Northeast would be half of the 90-degree measurement for East:

$$90 \div 2 = 45$$

Northeast is at 45 degrees.

With that example in mind, can you determine the other three combined directions—Southeast, Southwest, and Northwest?

Southeast is midway between East and South. To find the degree measure of Southeast, add up East and South and divide by two:

$$90 + 180 = 270$$
$$270 \div 2 = 135$$

Southeast is at approximately 135 degrees.

How about Southwest?

$$180 + 270 = 450$$
$$450 \div 2 = 225$$

Southwest is at 225 degrees.

And, finally, can you calculate the degrees for Northwest?

Northwest is a little tricky, since you may think that it is somewhere between 270 degrees and *zero* degrees. Remember, though, that one complete revolution is 360 degrees. Those are the two numbers you must use to calculate Northwest—270 degrees and 360 degrees:

$$270 + 360 = 630$$
$$630 \div 2 = 315$$

So Northwest is at roughly 315 degrees!

Here's our complete chart:

North – 0°

Northeast – 45°

East – 90°

Southeast – 135°

South – 180°

Southwest – 225°

West – 270°

Northwest – 315°

The Compass Rose

Sometimes maps will include a compass rose to indicate which way is north.

A compass rose is a **two-dimensional** representation of a compass. A compass rose, obviously, isn't functional. In other words, turning the map will not cause the compass rose to change position.

In older maps particularly, the compass rose is often highly stylized and decorated.

An example of a detailed compass rose

GLOBES, LONGITUDE, AND LATITUDE

Considering that the earth is round, doesn't it seem a little odd that many of the maps we use to represent the earth are flat?

Because it uses a round surface, or a sphere, to represent a round object, a globe is the most precise map of the earth available.

It seems odd because it is odd. The fact is, it's impossible to represent a round object like the earth on a flat map without creating a lot of **distortion**. Distortion causes some of the earth's continents to appear larger or smaller on a map than they really are.

The solution developed for this problem was to represent a round object—the earth—with another round object—*a globe!*

The earth and the globes used to represent the earth are all **spheres.**

In the last section, you learned about degrees and how they apply to the measurement of a circle. Degrees also apply to the measurement of spheres.

Have you ever cut an orange right down the middle? What happens?

That's right—you end up with two orange halves. That's a little bit like how the earth is divided up. Actually, it is divided up twice.

The first division takes place from North to South. Imagine a line starting from the North Pole, traveling through Great Britain, Europe, Africa, and down to Antarctica. This line is known as the prime meridian and it represents 0 degrees. Meanwhile, on the other side of the earth, the same line continues, only now it is no longer the prime meridian. Instead, it is called the 180-degree line.

This might seem confusing at first, but look at your compass again. Imagine that the compass is the earth viewed from above. If the center of the compass is the North Pole, then 0 degrees would be the line of the prime meridian, and the same line returning to the North Pole on the other side would be at 180 degrees!

All of the measurements in between the prime meridian and the 180-degree line are known as degrees of **longitude**. Degrees of longitude are represented by vertical, or up and down, lines.

You learned before that the earth is actually divided twice. The second dividing line measures around the earth like a belt. This line is called the equator. Again, the equator divides the earth in half and functions as 0 degrees. Meanwhile, the North Pole, the top of the world, would be at 90 degrees north while the South Pole, the bottom of the world, would be at 90 degrees south.

Every degree in between the equator and either of the earth's poles represents a measurement of **latitude**. Areas north of the equator are measured at degrees north latitude. Areas south of the equator are measured at degrees south latitude.

In between degrees of longitude or latitude are even smaller measurements called **minutes.** In every degree there are sixty minutes. If there are 90 degrees between the equator to the north pole, how many minutes is that?

You can find out by multiplying:

$$90 \times 60 = 5400$$

There are 5,400 minutes between the equator and the North Pole!

Any place on the earth can be located by specifying degrees and minutes of latitude and longitude. The symbol for degrees is °, while the symbol for minutes is ´.

Here, for instance, is the location of Bangor, a city in Maine:

City	State	Lat. °	Lat. ´	Long. °	Long. ´
Bangor	Maine	44	48	68	47

You can read this data as, 44 degrees 48 minutes North latitude, 68 degrees 47 minutes West longitude. The readings for most of the United States will be in degrees *north* latitude and *west* longitude. This is simply because the continent of North America is above, or north, of the equator and west of the prime meridian.

Take a look at some more cities of the United States located by latitude and longitude. Here is a list of five cities:

City	State	Lat. °	Lat. ´	Long. °	Long. ´
Montgomery	Alabama	32	22	86	18
Juneau	Alaska	58	18	134	25
Phoenix	Arizona	33	26	112	4
Little Rock	Arkansas	34	44	92	17
Sacramento	California	38	34	121	29

What if you were to compare the locations of the first two cities, Montgomery, Alabama, and Juneau, Alaska?

To start with, you probably already knew that Juneau, Alaska, is west of Montgomery, Alabama, but what if you wanted to find out exactly how far west?

Any location can be determined using degrees of longitude and latitude. For example, the city of Boston, pictured here, is located at 42° 22' North latitude and 71° 2' West longitude. How does that compare with the city of Bismarck, North Dakota, located at 46° 46' North latitude and 100° 45' West longitude?

One thing you can do to find out is compare the measurements of longitude for each city:

Juneau, Alaska: 134° 25´

Montgomery, Alabama: 86° 18´

Just to make things simpler, drop the minutes:

Juneau, Alaska: 134°

Montgomery, Alabama: 86°

Now subtract the smaller number from the larger number:

$$134 - 86 = 48°$$

So Juneau, Alaska, is about 48 degrees west of Montgomery, Alabama!

About how far north is Juneau, Alaska, compared to Montgomery, Alabama? To find out, compare the latitudes of each city, dropping the minutes:

Juneau, Alaska: 58°

Montgomery, Alabama: 32°

Then subtract the smaller number from the larger number:

$$58 - 32 = 26°$$

Juneau, Alaska, is 26 degrees north of Montgomery, Alabama!

Finally, when you put the readings for latitude and longitude together, you should be able to say that Juneau, Alaska, is roughly 48 degrees West, 26 degrees North of Montgomery, Alabama!

ELEVATION

Have you ever climbed a mountain? Maybe you and your family have done this on a summer vacation.

If you look at the right map, you can probably find the mountain you climbed. It will likely appear as a little triangle along with the mountain's height. You see, just as maps can be used to express distance and direction, they can also be used to express **elevation.**

Maps can also be used to specify elevation. If, for example, a map told you that the tallest mountain of this range reaches up 15,000 feet, what is it 15,000 feet **above***?*

The word *elevation* might remind you of the word *elevator*. That's a good association, actually, because an elevator takes you up.

Note that elevation is all a matter of comparison. In the case of an elevator, the floors are all being compared to the ground, or first, floor. For instance, the third floor of a building is two stories higher than the first floor.

Mountains are also measured in terms of elevation. But what are they being compared to? Unlike an elevator, there isn't really a first floor on a mountain!

The missing link here is **sea level.**

Sea level is pretty much what it sounds like—the level of the sea. Sea level isn't really a fixed number, so the approximate sea level is the starting point for measuring elevation. Sea level, then, is zero, and anything higher than sea level is above sea level.

To demonstrate, take a look at this chart showing the ten highest mountains in the United States:

Rank #	Name	State	Height (feet)
1	Mt. McKinley	Alaska	20,320
2	Mt. St. Elias	Alaska	18,008
3	Mt. Foraker	Alaska	17,400
4	Mt. Bona	Alaska	16,500
5	Mt. Blackburn	Alaska	16,390
6	Mt. Sanford	Alaska	16,237
7	Mt. Vancouver	Alaska	15,979
8	South Buttress	Alaska	15,885
9	Mt. Churchill	Alaska	15,638
10	Mt. Fairweather	Alaska	15,300

*Source: Infoplease.com

The fourth column is labeled, simply, "Height (feet)." But what it actually represents is feet above sea level. Mount McKinley, for instance, is 20,320 feet high. That means that Mount McKinley is 20,320 feet above sea level.

Mount St. Elias, on the other hand, rises up to 18,008 feet above sea level. How many more feet above sea level is Mount McKinley compared to Mount St. Elias?

You can find out by subtracting the smaller number from the larger number:

$$20320 - 18008 = 2312$$

Mount McKinley rises up about 2,312 more feet than Mount St. Elias!

What about the mountain in "tenth place," Mount Fairweather? Mount Fairweather rises up 15,300 feet above sea level. Can you compare Mount Fairweather to both Mount McKinley and Mount St. Elias?

First of all, compare Mount Fairweather's elevation with the elevation of Mount McKinley. Remember to subtract the smaller number from the larger number:

$$20320 - 15300 = 5020$$

Mount Fairweather is 5,020 feet lower than Mount McKinley!

Now compare Mount Fairweather with Mount St. Elias:

$$18008 - 15300 = 2708$$

Mount Fairweather is about 2,708 feet *lower* than Mount St. Elias!

Maybe you've noticed that all of these mountains are in the state of Alaska. What is the highest mountain peak in the United States that is not in Alaska?

The highest mountain in the United States that isn't in Alaska is Mount Whitney in California. Mount Whitney reaches up 14,494 feet above sea level. Compare that with the height of Mount McKinley.

$$20320 - 14494 = 5826$$

So, Mount Whitney is about 5,826 feet lower than Mount McKinley. Maybe so, but they're both still a lot of work to climb!

Measuring Sea Level

Sea level is something that is constantly changing. This is due to factors like temperature, rainfall, and the tides.

As you can imagine, all of these factors make determining the sea level extremely difficult. So how do scientists do it?

One method of finding the sea level is by using a device called a stilling well, which is really just a thick length of pipe with a hole in the middle. Even though the waters outside the pipe may shift, the water that drains into the pipe remains relatively stable, making a fairly accurate reading of the sea level possible. Scientists have also begun using satellites to calculate the sea level.

Neither of these methods is foolproof, but the readings they give us can be trusted within a small margin of error.

DEPTH

In the previous section, you learned about maps that describe elevation, like the elevation of mountains that rise up from sea level. Now you're going to learn about **depths**, or measurements that start at sea level and go down.

Above: In many ways, the world beneath sea level looks very much like another planet. This unusual creature, for instance, is not an alien being, but an example of a Ray—a species of fish that lives at the bottom of the sea.

Left: There is no such thing as a 100% accurate number for sea level. However, with the aid of special instruments like satellites and stilling wells, an approximate reading is possible.

There are four main oceans in the world: the Atlantic, Pacific, Arctic, and Indian. Here is a chart specifying the **average** depth and the greatest known depth for each ocean:

Ocean	Average Depth (Feet)	Greatest Known Depth (Feet)	Place of Greatest Known Depth
Pacific Ocean	13,215	36,198	Mariana Trench
Atlantic Ocean	12,880	30,246	Puerto Rico Trench
Indian Ocean	13,002	24,460	Sunda Trench
Arctic Ocean	3,953	18,456	77°45´N; 175°W

*Source - www.infoplease.com

In order to understand what this all means, you first have to learn about averages.

What if you went with your family to the beach tomorrow? Depending on where you live, you might end up at a beach facing the Atlantic or the Pacific Ocean. For this example, though, imagine you went to a beach on the Pacific Ocean.

If you went to the edge of that beach where the land meets the sea, the water there wouldn't be 13,000 feet deep. That is because 13,000 feet is just an average depth of the Pacific Ocean. An average is a number that represents a group of numbers.

Using the chart, can you figure out how much deeper the Pacific Ocean is compared to the Atlantic Ocean?

You can find out by subtracting the smaller number from the larger number:

$$13215 - 12880 = 335$$

So the average depth of the Pacific Ocean is roughly 335 feet below sea level deeper than the Atlantic Ocean!

On the other hand, the third column on the chart, the one labeled "Greatest Known Depth" is not an average. You can, however, compare the greatest depth of a particular ocean with the average depth of that ocean.

For instance, the deepest portion of the Indian Ocean is the Sunda Trench, which reaches down 24,460 feet below sea level. How much deeper is this compared to the average depth of the Indian Ocean, measured at 13,002 feet?

To find out, just subtract the smaller number from the larger number:

$$24460 - 13002 = 11458$$

The Sunda Trench reaches down 11,458 feet below sea level deeper than the average depth of the Indian Ocean!

The greatest depth in the entire ocean, though, is the Mariana Trench, located in the Pacific Ocean. This trench reaches down 36,198 feet below sea level.

In one mile there are 5,280 feet. How many miles below sea level, then, does the Mariana Trench reach?

You can find out by dividing the depth of the Mariana Trench by the number of feet in one mile:

$$36198 \div 5280 = 6.85$$

So, the Mariana Trench reaches almost seven miles down below sea level!

Fathoms

Sometimes, the sea is also measured in terms of **fathoms**. A fathom is an old unit of measurement that is equal to six feet.

How deep is the Mariana Trench in terms of fathoms?

You can find out by dividing the measurement for the trench in feet by the number of feet in one fathom:

$$36198 \div 6 = 6033$$

The Mariana Trench is about 6,033 fathoms deep!

If the pool pictured here has a depth of fifteen feet at its deepest point, how many fathoms is that equal to? How many fathoms deep do you think the sea behind the pool is?

THE SOLAR SYSTEM

Did you know that maps can also be used to represent outer space? If you have ever looked at a map of our solar system you already understand this.

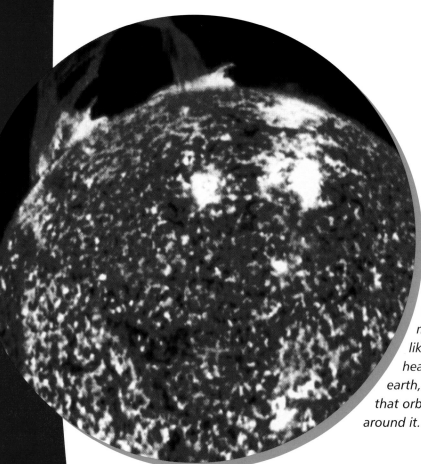

Do you know what a solar system is? "Solar" is really just a fancy name for the sun. A solar system is made up of a star, like the sun that heats our planet earth, and the planets that orbit, or circle, around it.

Don't forget that maps are primarily used for navigation. And, just as mankind has explored the planet Earth, the human race is only just beginning to explore outer space. Space is a pretty big place, but maps help to make it understandable.

Can you name the nine planets of our solar system? Here they are, in order of increasing distance from the sun:

Mercury

Venus

Earth

Mars

Jupiter

Saturn

Uranus

Neptune

Pluto

What is the distance of each of these planets from the sun?

Once you leave the earth, there is no point in measuring distances in terms of miles. Things in outer space are so far apart that miles are simply too short a unit of measurement. Instead, scientists measure space distances in terms of astronomical units (AU).

The astronomical unit is based on the distance from the sun to the earth. This distance is approximately equal to 92.9 million miles. As a number, that would look like this: 92,900,000 miles.

Here are the distances for the remaining planets in terms of astronomical units. You'll notice that both Mercury and Venus are less than one astronomical unit away from the sun, since they are closer to it than the planet Earth:

Mercury – .04 AU

Venus – .07 AU

Earth – 1 AU

Mars – 1.5 AU

Jupiter – 5.2 AU

Saturn – 9.6 AU

Uranus – 19.2 AU

Neptune – 30.1 AU

Pluto – 39.4 AU

How far away from Earth is the ninth planet, Pluto?

You can find out by comparing each planet's astronomical unit measure. Just subtract the smaller number from the larger number:

$$39.4 - 1 = 38.4$$

Pluto is 38.4 astronomical units away from the Earth.

What if, though, you wanted to know each planet's distance away from the sun in miles?

All you would have to do is multiply the planet's astronomical unit measure by the number of miles in one astronomical unit (92.9 million):

Mercury – .04 AU x 92,900,000

Venus – .07 AU x 92,900,000

Earth – 1 AU x 92,900,000

Mars – 1.5 AU x 92,900,000

Jupiter – 5.2 AU x 92,900,000

Saturn – 9.6 AU x 92,900,000

Uranus – 19.2 AU x 92,900,000

Neptune – 30.1 AU x 92,900,000

Pluto – 39.4 AU x 92,900,000

Notice anything strange about this globe? That's because it is actually a map of the moon, not the earth! As you can see, the moon does not have any oceans. It does, however, have a number of deep craters.

Now calculate the results. Are you sure you're ready? These are going to be some big numbers!

Mercury – 3,716,000 miles from the sun

Venus – 6,503,000 miles from the sun

Earth – 92,900,000 miles from the sun

Mars – 139,350,000 miles from the sun

Jupiter – 483,080,000 miles from the sun

Saturn – 891,840,000 miles from the sun

Uranus – 1,783,680,000 miles from the sun

Neptune – 2,796,290,000 miles from the sun

Pluto – 3,660,260,000 miles from the sun

Now you know why it's easier for scientists to measure distances in space with astronomical units!

The Tenth Planet?

For some time now, scientists have been theorizing that there may be a tenth planet in our solar system.

This tenth planet has never actually been seen, mainly because it is so far away from the sun that very little light reaches it. It is estimated that this planet is roughly 3 trillion miles away from the sun, which would be

3,000,000,000,000

What would that be equal to in astronomical units?

$$3,000,000,000,000 \div 92,900,000 = 32292.78$$

The tenth planet is roughly 32,293 astronomical units away from the sun!

A tenth planet would certainly change the maps of our solar system a great deal. For one thing, a name will have to be decided on. What would you call the tenth planet?

CONCLUSION

After reading this book, you may be left with one last question—who is responsible for creating all the maps that people depend on to guide them?

People who research, design, and create maps are called **cartographers.** Meanwhile, the science of creating maps is known as **cartography.**

If you have found this book interesting, maybe you will want to consider a career in cartography! You can be part of the future of mapmaking. Maybe you'll create maps of portions of the ocean that people never knew existed, or even maps detailing the surface of other planets!

All you need is math!

Pictured here is an "old world" map with some of the navigational tools used in ancient times.

THE METRIC SYSTEM

We actually have two systems of weights and measure in the United States. Quarts, pints, gallons, ounces, and pounds are all units of the U.S. Customary System, also known as the English System.

The other system of measurement, and the only one sanctioned by the United States Government, is the metric system, which is also known as the International System of Units. French scientists developed the metric system in the 1790s. One basic unit of measurement in the metric system is the meter, which is about one ten-millionth the distance from the North Pole to the equator.

A metal bar used to represent the length of the standard meter was even created. This bar was replaced in the 1980s, though, when scientists changed the standard of measurement for the meter to a portion of the distance traveled by light in a vacuum.

Most of the world uses the metric system. In terms of maps, this usually means that distances are measured not in miles, but in kilometers. One mile is equal to 1.6094 kilometers.

The calculations for metric measurement are a simple matter of multiplication. For instance, you already know that the United States is about 2,700 miles across. How many kilometers is that?

$$1.6093 \times 2700 = 4345.11$$

The United States is about 4,345 kilometers across!

You calculated that the Mariana Trench reached about 6.85 miles below sea level. How many kilometers is that? To find out, multiply:

$$6.85 \times 1.6093 = 11.024$$

The Mariana Trench reaches down about 11 kilometers!

You can try some of these calculations for yourself by going through this book again and converting the standard measurements to their metric equivalents.

Try it!

GLOSSARY

Area – A measure of the total land mass in a space

Average – A number used to represent a group of numbers

Cartographers – People who design and create maps

Cartography – The science of designing and creating maps

Degrees – Very small divisions of a circle

Depths – Measurements below sea level

Direction – The line along which something moves

Distance – The space between two places

Distortion – Error

Elevation – Height; measurements above sea level

Fathoms – A measure of depth equal to six feet

Latitude – Horizontal degrees of measurement

Legend – A reference explaining what the symbols on a map represent

Longitude – Vertical degrees of measurement

Minutes – Smaller divisions of degrees; one degree is equal to 60 minutes

Multiples – The result of multiplying a single number by a series of other numbers

Navigation – The process of directing people or crafts

Revolution – One full circle; 360 degrees

Scale – A smaller measurement of distance used to represent a larger measurement of distance

Sea Level – The level of the sea; the point from which both height and depth are measured

Spheres – Round objects

Two-Dimensional – Length and height, but not width or depth

Further Reading

Ashcroft, Minnie. *Marvelous Map Activities for Young Learners*. Scholastic, 2002.

The Blackbirch Kid's Visual Reference of the World. Blackbirch, 2001.

Zeman, Anne and Kate Kelly. *Everything You Need To Know About Math Homework*. Scholastic, 1994.

Websites to Visit

www.mapquest.com
Map Quest

http://www.nypl.org/research/chss/epo/mapexhib/map.html
New York Public Library – How To Read a Map

http://www.howstuffworks.com/compass.htm
How Stuff Works – How Compasses Work

http://abcnews.go.com/sections/science/DailyNews/
planet991007.html
ABC News – Tenth Planet

http://www.infoplease.com/ipa/A0001796.html
Infoplease – Latitude and Longitude of U.S. and
Canadian Cities

INDEX

About the Author

Kieran Walsh has written a variety of children's nonfiction books, primarily on historical and social studies topics, including the recent Rourke series *Holiday Celebrations* and *Countries In the News*. He divides his time between upstate New York and New York City.